In Year 6 you HAVE to do SATs, whether you like it or not

Writing's one of the toughest things you have to do in the SATs.
Don't panic — we're here to show you exactly what you need to do.

THIS BOOK

Writing Rules tells you
how to tackle *every* typ
of writing you might b
asked to do in the SAT

D1637795

You can get loads of <u>practice</u> on all the types of writing
covered in this book in the four <u>Writing Workbooks</u>:

WORKBOOK 1 — FICTION WRITING

* HORROR STORIES
* ADVENTURE STORIES
* FABLES
* STORIES WITH FLASHBACKS
* FANTASY ADVENTURES
* PLAY SCRIPTS
* STORIES WITH A FAMILIAR SETTING

KS2 English SAT BUSTER — Workbook 1 Fiction Writing

WORKBOOK 3 — NON-FICTION WRITING

* FACTUAL REPORTS
* LETTERS TO FRIENDS AND FAMILY
* FORMAL LETTERS
* ADVERTS, FLYERS
* DIARIES
* DISCUSSING ISSUES
* WRITING ABOUT YOUR POINT OF VIEW

KS2 English SAT BUSTER — Workbook 3 Non-Fiction Writing

WORKBOOK 2 — FICTION WRITING

* STORIES THAT RAISE ISSUES
* MYSTERY STORIES
* CONVERSATIONS
* HISTORICAL STORIES
* SCIENCE FICTION STORIES
* HUMOROUS STORIES
* STORIES WITH A DILEMMA
* STORIES WITH A TWIST

KS2 English SAT BUSTER — Workbook 2 Fiction Writing

WORKBOOK 4 — NON-FICTION WRITING

* WRITING AN ARGUMENT
* RECOUNTING EVENTS
* ARTICLES
* BIOGRAPHIES
* NEWSLETTERS
* INSTRUCTIONS
* DESCRIPTIONS
* EXPLANATIONS

KS2 English SAT BUSTER — Workbook 4 Non-Fiction Writing

Contents

Non-Fiction Writing

FICTION WRITING

Horror Stories

A good horror story should make readers jump out of their seats with fright.
The monsters are often traditional things, like vampires, but make up your own if you want.

RULES FOR A GREAT HORROR STORY...

- *Choose a spooky setting, like a run-down fairground or an old, empty house*
- *Have an unusual ghost or monster as a main character*
- *Build up the suspense with descriptive words, short sentences and cliff-hangers*
- *End with a surprise*

Here's a SAT-style <u>horror story</u> question...

> The secret of the haunted sports hall has been kept quiet for years,
> but it seems that the secret is about to be revealed.
>
> **Write a short story based on this idea.**
>
> You will need to decide:
> - What is haunting the sports hall
> - What happens to the victims
> - How the problem is stopped

Plan your story before you write it.

This is where you decide what your horror story is going to be like.
Think about what will scare the reader and build up suspense.

Who or **what** is haunting the sports hall?
A vampire.

What does it **look like**?
Scarred from the sun, big, white fangs, smelly, very frightening.

Make monsters, ghosts and evil characters look really nasty.

Who are the **victims**?
A group of teenagers exploring the old sports hall.

Is the ending **happy** or **sad**? What happens?
Both — the vampire dies but it has bitten one of the group.

Give readers the heebie-jeebies by making something unexpected happen at the end.

Horror Stories

Once you've got your plan, you should be able to write a really horrible horror story. In the main part of the story, crank up the suspense, then finish with an exciting ending.

As the giggling teenagers entered the empty sports hall, the creature watching them melted into the shadows. Nervously, the two girls in the group dared each other to scream and scare their boyfriends.

In the first paragraph, set the scene and introduce the main characters.

"This is rubbish! Who said this place was haunted? There's nothing but mice and a few manky tennis balls. I'm off!" said the tallest boy. As he turned to pick up a ball from the floor, he heard a sound behind him.

Use short sentences, when you want to build up suspense.

"Stop messing about, you lot!" he laughed, but when he turned around he was alone. He dropped the ball but it didn't bounce. Then the creature spoke.

Its cold voice filled the room as it moved forward into the moonlight. Terror seized the boy. He tried to run but he was being held by the icy grip of the creature.

You can show how characters feel in the way they talk.

"Before I suck your blood, I will give you a sporting chance!" it boomed. "W..w..what do you mean?" stuttered the boy, staring at the creature's huge white fangs.
"Let's see if you can outrun me," the creature shouted and picked the boy up clear of the ground.

Paint a really clear picture of the nasty characters — it keeps readers gripped.

As he was being lifted, the boy noticed the scarring on the creature's hands and face, as if it had been burned. It smelt as though it had been living underground.

The boy was flung across the room. As soon as he hit the ground, he got up and ran. Then he remembered the three friends he had left behind. He turned and ran back to the hall to save them but stopped in his tracks. His three friends were running towards him and the creature was chasing them!

As the creature ran, the morning sun peeped over the horizon. The light touched the creature. It frazzled and fell to the floor in a pile of ash. The children hugged each other and sobbed with relief, as the police arrived.

"You've had a lucky escape," said the officer, "but you're alright now."

"I wish that were true," thought the youngest girl as the ambulance drove them away, but she knew what the bite on her neck meant and she dreaded nightfall for fear of what she might do.

Don't forget the surprise at the end.

Adventure Stories

A good adventure story should be unbearably exciting. The characters are usually on a journey where lots of things happen to them along the way. Most have happy endings.

RULES FOR A GREAT ADVENTURE STORY...

- *Have some kind of problem that forces the characters to go on a journey*
- *Think up some dangers that they come across on the journey*
- *Think of original ways that the characters overcome the dangers they meet*
- *Build up suspense through a series of adventures, each one worse than the last*

Here's a SAT-style <u>adventure story</u> question...

It is the middle of winter in the snowy hills of Colorado and Mike Stone's grandfather has fallen ill. The only place to get help is thirty miles away, through the snow-filled valley. The telephone lines are down and a blizzard is blowing in, so everything relies on Mike.

Write an adventure story based on this idea.

You will need to decide:
- What Mike takes with him
- Who goes with him
- Three dangers they meet along the way
- How they overcome them

Make a plan before you write your story.

Who goes on the adventure?
Mike Stone, his friends, Alfie and Greg, Buck the Alsatian.

Make the main characters likeable so readers will care what happens to them.

Where are they are going?
Through a snowstorm to the nearest village.

What three **problems** do they come across?
Wolves, bear trap, avalanche.

Make each problem worse than the last, to build up the tension.

How do they solve the problems and **what happens** in the end?
Dog chases wolf away, they dodge the avalanche and manage to escape from the bear trap. They get to the village and fetch help.

© CGP 200

Adventure Stories

Now you can use your plan to produce a fantastic adventure story. The most important thing to do is make it exciting with surprises and disasters all along the journey.

The icy wind whistled in from the East. The small Colorado ranch was covered in a blanket of snow that made it look a Christmas card. Only a small rectangle of yellow light from the window showed there was any life inside.

Bring in some dangers in the very first paragraph.

Inside the ranch, ten year old Mike Stone, his two friends Alfie and Greg, and Buck, his Alsatian, were looking out of the window at the growing snow drift that threatened to cover them entirely. As they gazed they heard a groan.

Introduce the characters early on.

Behind them, Mike's grandad was lying on the ground clutching his stomach. "It's my stomach again and I've no medicine left! If I don't get some soon, I'm going to die for sure!"

Bring in a dramatic problem that needs to be sorted out.

Without hesitation the boys ran to the kitchen and started filling their bags with food, blankets, a torch and matches. They put on their thickest coats and started checking their maps. "The nearest town is thirty miles away..." Mike started, but before he had time to finish his sentence, Buck had burst through the door and their unforgettable journey had begun.

As soon as the journey starts, describe an exciting and dangerous situation.

The snowstorm was getting stronger as they pushed on. After only a mile, Buck started snarling.

"What's wrong, boy?" asked Alfie. He didn't have to wait for an answer. Out of the snow-covered trees peeped the snout of a wolf.

Buck launched forward like a torpedo and jumped on the wolf. The two animals snapped and growled, nipped and scratched, until the wolf realised the battle was lost and scuttled off into the trees. The three boys ran to greet their friend. They hugged him to thank him for being so brave.

Fit in as many dangerous situations as you can.

The rest of the journey brought more dangers. An avalanche nearly covered them all, but fortunately Greg saw it in time before it hit them. A rusty bear trap caught Alfie's boot, but it didn't break his skin and they managed to pull him out. After a long night of walking they finally made it to the village and raised the alarm.

An air ambulance set off to save Mike's grandad, with the three boys and Buck safely inside, wrapped in warm blankets.

Solve the big problem at the end and give your adventure story a happy ending.

Fables

A fable is a fiction story that teaches the readers a lesson.
The characters in fables are often talking animals.

RULES FOR A GREAT FABLE...

- *Base the story round a moral (a lesson for the readers)*
- *Use animals as characters*
- *Include simple conversations between characters*
- *Have a simple beginning, middle and end*
- *Choose a title that explains the story*

Here's a SAT-style <u>fable</u> question...

> **Write a fable that tells the reader how the leopard got his spots.**
>
> You will need to decide:
> - What animals are involved in the story
> - What type of language is used in the fable
> - How the leopard got his spots and whether it was
>   for good or bad reasons

Always work out what your story is going to be about <u>before</u> you start writing.

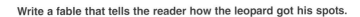

What is the leopard **like** in your story?	**What happens** to the leopard?
He's rude to other animals and a show-off. *Think hard about this bit. If the main character's interesting, it makes the whole story interesting.*	*He gets covered in black spots that dry so hard in the sun that they never come off.*
What other animals are there? **How** do they deal with the leopard? *Gazelle, eagle, snake, birds, giraffe. They make him believe he's caught a disease because of his bad attitude.*	**Does** he change his ways at the end? *Not really — he finds it too hard to be nice, so he's still rude and the spots stay on him.*

© CGP 200

Fables

*Now you can put together a top-class fable. It's fine if it's not very realistic
— so long as it's got a strong moral that's clear to the readers.*

<u>HOW DID LEOPARD GET HIS SPOTS?</u>

> Give your fable a simple title that says exactly what the story's about.

Leopard was a rude creature who told lies and showed off to get attention. He bragged, made up stories and generally upset the other animals.

> At the beginning, say what the main character is like.

"I don't know why Leopard shows off so much," said Gazelle. "He doesn't have horns, like me."

"Nor can he fly high, like me," said Eagle. "So why does he show off so much?"

> Tell some of the story with speech.

"I've got an idea," said Snake, the wisest creature of them all. "Let's teach him a lesson."

The animals huddled together and hatched a plan. Every time he was rude, the animals would paint a black spot onto his fur as he slept. They would tell Leopard he had caught a disease that only rude creatures caught and the spots wouldn't go away until he stopped being rude.

The next day Leopard awoke and was rude to the birds.

"Stop singing so loudly this morning — you're out of tune!" he snapped.
During his morning nap, the birds each painted a black spot on to his fur.

Just before lunch, Leopard woke up and was rude to the giraffes.

"It's no wonder your necks are so long, Giraffe, your feet smell terrible!" he growled.
During his afternoon nap, the giraffes each painted a black spot onto his fur.

The following morning Leopard saw the spots on his fur.

"My beautiful coat! I'm dying, I'm dying!" he yelped.

"No you're not," said Snake, "You've caught bad temper disease. The spots will go when you start being nice."

"What do you know, stupid Snake!" snarled Leopard. The wise snake chuckled as he slithered away.

Leopard tried to be nice but he found it too difficult. By the end of the day he was back to being rude, and the sun had dried the spots onto his fur.

> Put the moral right at the end.

The spots never disappeared — he was stuck with them forever. But you know what they say — a leopard can't change his spots, and now you know why.

Stories With Flashbacks

In a flashback, the story jumps back in time, to tell readers a little bit extra about the main characters or the plot. Flashbacks are ace — they can really improve your stories.

RULES FOR A GREAT FLASHBACK STORY...

- *In flashbacks, write about the character at an earlier time in their life*
- *Use flashbacks to help readers understand what's happening in the story*
- *Only use flashbacks once or twice, so that they're effective*
- *Write flashbacks in the past tense*

Here's a SAT-style flashback question...

> As Captain Hallas approached the oil rig under the cover of darkness, he knew what he had to do. He remembered the advice his father gave him just before he died. Those wise words never left him and he needed them now more than ever.
>
> **Write an adventure story that uses a flashback to help the reader to understand the story better. Follow on from the sentences above.**
>
> You will need to decide:
> - When to include the flashback
> - What to include in the flashback
> - How it will help the reader to understand the story

If you get a writing frame, use it to get your ideas straight before you start.

Where does the story take place?	**When** does the flashback take place?
On an oil rig in the Atlantic Ocean that has been captured by rebel soldiers.	*Just before the hero begins his attack.*
	Put your flashback at an exciting moment to add suspense.
What is the flashback?	**How** does the flashback affect the story?
His father's words of advice.	*The flashback explains why the character is so determined to stop the rebels.*
	Make something happen in the flashback to explain what is happening now.

© CGP 200

Stories With Flashbacks

Now you've got your main ideas together, you can produce a brilliant story with flashbacks.
*You can use flashbacks in **any** type of story.*

The night was thick and black. Captain Hallas could not see the oil rig but he could hear the rebels muttering as they patrolled the landing platforms. Every now and then he paddled a little to keep his boat close to the rig. All the time his eyes were straining for the signal. Barney would flash his torch as soon as it was safe to join him on the rig.

Hallas checked the time. Midnight already. His watch was the one his father had worn... ◄— **Make it clear where the flashback starts.**

Hallas was ten years old. Flies buzzed in and out of the broken hospital window. His father was dying. He had been shot, fighting rebels in the jungle. The dying man leant forward and hugged the boy. ◄ **Use *your* flashbacks to explain the main story.**

"Son," he said in a cracked voice. "There are two types of people in the world — good and bad. It's up to us to stop the bad ones getting their way. I may not be around to fight them any longer, but you are. Don't let the bad guys win, son." With those words, his father closed his eyes and passed away.

The boy broke down in tears. He swore to himself he would live by his father's dying words... ◄ **Stop the flashback suddenly and go back to the main story.**

A torch flashed in the distance. Hallas's attention snapped back to the present. That was the code: two short flashes, then two long. He paddled swiftly towards the light.

At the rig, Barney was waiting. He showed Hallas two rebel soldiers, handcuffed to a pipe, then crept towards a lighted window. Hallas followed. Inside, more rebels were playing cards. Five hostages were lying in chains on the floor.

Hallas signalled to Barney. Barney crept up to the window, then smashed his fists against the glass. The rebels dashed outside and Barney ran for his life. Hallas slipped into the room and unchained the hostages.

Barney was at the boat. The hostages tumbled in and Hallas dropped in after them. As the rebel soldiers reached the landing platform, the boat roared away from the rig.

"They'll be there for a while," Barney said. "I sank every last boat on the rig."

"Good work, Barney," said Captain Hallas. "Good work."

Stories With Flashbacks

Fantasy Adventures

Fantasy adventure stories are adventure stories set in a made-up world.
They usually include weird creatures like fairies and _very_ evil baddies.

RULES FOR A GREAT FANTASY ADVENTURE STORY...

- Base your story on a quest (a journey to find something or someone)
- Set your story in a made-up place
- Have some main characters who aren't human — the weirder the better
- Include some difficult challenges for the main characters to face

Here's a SAT-style _fantasy adventure story_ question...

> Blakely has been captured by the evil High Lords and put to work as a slave in a
> salt mine. He escapes and starts a journey back to his home in Little Hamlet.
> On his way home, Blakely meets a friendly creature and is nearly captured.
>
> **Write a fantasy adventure based on this idea.**
>
> You will need to decide:
> - How Blakely escapes from the salt mine
> - Who the friendly creature is
> - What happens when Blakely is nearly captured
> - How the story ends

Plan your story before you write it.

How does Blakely **escape** from the salt mine?
Blakely is in the mine, when he sees a spot of daylight through the salt. While the High Lord in charge of the mine is punishing another slave he digs a small hole in the salt and escapes.

Who is the **friendly creature** that Blakely meets?
Blakely hides in a cave and finds a cave monster there. The cave monster seems friendly and gives Blakely food.

> Make some of the characters imaginary.

How is Blakely **nearly captured**?
The cave monster is greedy. He says he'll help Blakely but instead leads him towards a High Lord town so he can get a reward. When Blakely realises, they have a fight.

> Put in a twist or two to make it more exciting.

How does the story **end**?....._Blakely reaches home safely._................

> Blakely's quest is getting home.

© CGP 200i

Fantasy Adventures

Once you've planned the story, you'll be ready to write a brilliant fantasy adventure.
Take a look at the example below and all the handy hints in the boxes.

"Keep working, you foolish small-brains," yelled the High Lord. "Don't you dare stop. If this mine doesn't produce 20 tonnes of salt in the next hour I will kill you all personally." One of the slaves sighed. The High Lord heard it.

Make the baddies *really* evil.

"Slave 3207, how dare you sigh! Aren't you happy working in the salt mine?" The High Lord took the trembling slave by the toes and dragged him down the tunnel towards the Small Cell of Punishment.

The other slaves didn't dare stop working. A small slave (number 1289), called Blakely, hacked miserably at the salt wall. Suddenly he saw daylight. He hacked away at the salt faster, his heart thumping. He could escape!

Get onto the quest as quickly as you can.

Blakely climbed through the hole and started to fall down a long, deep hole. Later on, he woke up in the dark, too tired to remember what had happened. His arm was bleeding and all he could think about was food. In the distance he hear the High Lord police shouting. He crawled further into the cave.

"Hello," said a voice. Blakely froze, but it was a friendly voice. He peered into the darkness. Blakely laughed, relieved. It was a cave monster and cave monsters are famous for their hospitality.

"Have you got any food?" croaked Blakely. And so Blakely and the cave monster shared a good meal of potato skins, pumpkin seeds and woodlice before going to sleep.

The next morning the cave monster showed Blakely which way he should go to get back to his home in Little Hamlet.

Don't let things go too smoothly. Throw in a surprising setback.

"I'll come with you, if you like," said the cave monster. Blakely couldn't believe his luck. As they walked along they talked happily. Then Blakely stopped — ahead of them was a small town, with the High Lord flag flying from the gatepost. The cave monster had betrayed him and had taken him back to the High Lord!

"Reward!" said the cave monster, grabbing Blakely, "You wouldn't stop your friend getting a little reward?" Blakely screamed. He kicked the monster to the floor and bit its arm. The monster's grip loosened and Blakely ran. Fear gave him speed. He sprinted over hills and down the valley, safely back to Little Hamlet. No-one would catch him this time.

Play Scripts

A play script is basically the lines that actors speak when they are acting. A script also includes stage directions and instructions for the actors on how to say their lines.

RULES FOR A GREAT PLAY SCRIPT...

- Make sure most of what you write is what people actually say
- Describe the setting and how the actors should speak the lines
- <u>Don't</u> put speech marks around spoken words
- Tell the story through what the characters say

Here's a SAT-style <u>play script</u> question...

> Gabrielle and James are searching for their lost cat, Pumpkin, when they make a discovery that will change their lives forever.
>
> **Continue the scene below where Gabrielle and James follow Pumpkin's tail under a fence.**
>
> <u>SCENE 1</u>   *Down a side street off the main road. Saturday morning around 10.30am. Gabrielle and James are arguing.*
> Gabrielle: Why did you leave the gate open, stupid?
> James: It wasn't me, and anyway, you've left it open loads of times.
> Gabrielle: Well I didn't this time...what's that over there? *(looking at a broken fence)*
> James: Pumpkin! Slow down! *(Cat's tail disappears under the broken fence.)*

Make a plan before you write your play script.

What do the children **find** behind the fence?
A tunnel into a mysterious cave, where they find a bank robber's fortune.

Think of something unusual or exciting.

Who lives behind the fence?
A tramp.

Think of a character who's quite different to Gabrielle and James.

What happens to Gabrielle and James?
They fetch the police and they are given a large reward.

What happens to Pumpkin?
He gets a large fish to eat.

© CGP 200.

Play Scripts

Once you've done your plan, you can write a top-notch play script.
Use the speeches to make it as dramatic as possible.

Gabrielle: Come on, let's follow him, quick.

(The children climb over the fence.)

> Use stage directions to show what the characters do and how they feel.

James :   Where are we? I don't remember this cave being here before.
Gabrielle: Well, Pumpkin has disappeared into it, so lets keep moving. (anxiously)

(The children cautiously make their way into the cave.)
James: Are... Are... Are you sure Gabby? It looks a bit spooky.
Gabrielle: Don't be silly James and anyway, we need to rescue Pumpkin.
James: What was that?!

(Out of the shadows, steps a tramp stroking Pumpkin.)

> Bring in another character when you want something new to happen.

Gabrielle and James: (Delighted)   PUMPKIN!

(They run over to Pumpkin and stroke him.)
Gabrielle: Oh thank you, thank you, however can we thank you?
Tramp: Think nothing of it, he's a lovely cat. (handing Pumpkin over)
James: Do you live here?
Tramp: Yes I do. I've lived here for years.
James: (curious) But how come I've never seen this cave before?
Tramp: (whispering and leaning forward) Because you can only see it when the wind
            blows in the right direction!
James: (puzzled) OK...
Tramp: No really. You see, this cave can only be seen by lucky people.
Gabrielle: I've got to be honest, I don't feel very lucky. It's cold, damp and a
            spider has just crawled down my sock.
Tramp: Yes, but if you look there, you'll see that you're in fact very lucky. (pointing)
Gabrielle: Look, it's money, and lots of it!
Tramp: Oh it's money alright, and I know who put it there.
James: (excitedly) Who? Who?
Tramp: Well, last week the High Street bank was robbed. I saw the robbers and told
            them about this magic cave and they stashed it here. When they came back,
            though, the cave was gone and they've been searching ever since.
Gabrielle: Is there a reward?
Tramp: Oh yes, £500!
James: Well, what are we waiting for?!

(Runs towards mouth of cave and returns with the bank manager and a police officer.)
Bank Manager: My money! Please accept this reward.

(Hands over the money to Gabrielle.)
James: Fantastic! We can buy a big fish for Pumpkin (he pauses and looks at
            Pumpkin) ...and a new lock for the gate!

(They all laugh as they make their way out of the cave.)

> Never ever _ever_ use speech marks in a play script.

Stories With A Familiar Setting

In stories with familiar settings, unusual things
happen to ordinary people in ordinary places.

RULES FOR A GREAT STORY WITH A FAMILIAR SETTING...

- *Set the story in ordinary places*
- *Have ordinary people as your main characters*
- *Write about unusual or surprising events*
- *Include detailed descriptions to make the story convincing*

Here's a SAT-style question for a <u>story with a familiar setting</u>...

> Jake awoke to the sound of the alarm clock as usual and began to get
> dressed for school. 'Another boring day of SATs revision ahead,' he thought,
> but as he opened the new packet of Crazy Pops and poured them into his
> bowl, he realised that it wasn't going to be a boring day after all….
>
> **Continue the story. Make sure it is set in a familiar place.**
>
> You will need to consider:
> - What Jake finds in his cereal
> - How it affects his day
> - Who the other characters in the story are

Always work out what your story is going to be about <u>before</u> you start writing.

What does Jake find in his cereal?
He finds a large silver egg.

Who else is in the story?
Charlie and Sam (Jake's friends) and Mr Waddle (the school caretaker)

How does Jake's discovery **affect** the characters in the story?
It flashes with light and stops time, and freezes everybody in the school yard. The caretaker is standing in the shade when the second flash of light comes. He stays frozen.

How does the story **end**?
They rescue the caretaker and throw the egg in the canal to get rid of it.

The question gives you the ordinary setting. It's up to you to think of the <u>unusual</u> bits.

© CGP 200.

Stories With A Familiar Setting

Now you can use your ideas to write an amazing story.
Start with everything ordinary and normal, then bring in the strange events...

He was expecting a cheap plastic toy, but instead a large silvery egg splashed into his bowl. Jake fished the egg out and studied it. It was a perfectly formed egg made of a silvery substance. As he held it, he could feel its warmth and was certain there was movement inside.

> **Bring in your first unusual event straightaway.**

He didn't have any idea what the silver egg did, but it wasn't too long before he found out. As soon as he was in the school yard he ran up to his friends Charlie and Sam.

> **Set your story in familiar places like school and home.**

"Did you eat Crazy Pops this morning and have you got your silver egg?" he asked.

"Yes, I had Crazy Pops," said Charlie, "but I got a cheap plastic badge."

Jake showed them the silvery egg. It shimmered in the sunlight. Suddenly, a blinding flash shot into the sky and the boys found themselves standing, staring at the playground. Everybody and everything had frozen in time. People were standing with their mouths open in the middle of a conversation, or in mid-air as they jumped over a skipping rope.

> **Make your descriptions detailed — it makes the story more believable.**

As they stood in amazement, the sunlight caught the silver egg again and the same flash of light surrounded them. When they looked up, the playground had returned to normal and life carried on. Or so they thought...

When they were lining up, Charlie noticed Mr Waddle, the school caretaker, standing perfectly motionless in the shade of a large oak tree. He was bending to pick up a piece of litter. The boys ran over to the caretaker and Jake fished the silver egg out his pocket. This time there was no flash at all.

"It's the sunlight!" exclaimed Sam. "It only works in sunlight and Mr Waddle is in the shade!"

The boys picked up the frozen caretaker up and struggled over to the sunlit grass with him. They hid from view and Jake tried again. This time there was a flash of light from the egg and Mr Waddle was surprised to find that he wasn't under the tree any more.

"I think this could be dangerous if it fell into the wrong hands," said Jake.

That night the boys wrapped the egg in a sock and threw it into the canal.

"An ordinary ending to an extraordinary day," thought Jake, as he made his back home.

Stories That Raise Issues

*Stories that raise issues are about problems like loneliness, divorce and bullying.
They're often written from the point of view of the person with the problem.*

RULES FOR A GREAT ISSUE-RAISING STORY...

- Choose an issue that lots of people know about
- Begin by introducing the main character, then their problem
- Have a familiar setting
- Write in the first person (write as 'I') so you go into the main character's emotions
- Have a happy ending, where the problem is sorted out

Here's a SAT-style question for a __story that raises issues__...

> Hannah is upset. Bullies at her primary school are making her life a misery and she doesn't know why they are doing it.
>
> **Write a story about this from Hannah's point of view.**
>
> You will need to decide:
> - How old Hannah is
> - Who is bullying her and why
> - Who Hannah feels she can ask for help
> - How the problem is solved

If you get a writing frame, use it to get your ideas straight before you start.

Who is bullying Hannah and **why**?

Girls from Year 6 are bullying her because her Dad died recently.

Try and think what would really happen and write about that.

How are they bullying her?

Name calling, text messages, fighting, take her friends, whisper behind her back.

Describe the bullying in detail to make readers think about it.

Who does Hannah **tell**?

Eventually she tells her big sister, who tells her teacher.

How is the problem **stopped**?

The main bully confesses and says that she is bullied by her sister.

© CGP 200?

Stories That Raise Issues

Turn the ideas from your plan into a top issue-raising story.
Make it as realistic as you can.

My name is Hannah and I am nine years old. I live in Manchester, with my Mum and my elder sister. My Mum takes us all out every week. Sometimes we go shopping and sometimes we go to the cinema, but wherever we go it's always good fun. Sometimes I can bring a friend and I usually bring my best friend Gemma.

First introduce the main character. Then say what their problem is.

I love the weekend, but as Sunday night approaches I get very, very low. Monday morning means school. I used to love school, running and dancing in the yard. But then my Dad died and all of a sudden people would say the cruellest things. At first it was no-one in particular, but then Nicola and Rebecca from Year 6 started calling me names every day. I couldn't quite believe it at first — I'd done nothing to them. Then they got my mobile phone number and they started to send me really nasty text messages. I had to turn my phone off at the weekends so they couldn't spoil it.

Set your story in a school or a local street — somewhere really normal.

The worst thing they did was steal my friends so I had no-one to play with, apart from Gemma that is. One morning we had an assembly by some actors all about bullying. They asked us how bullying made us feel but I didn't want to speak. I didn't want anyone to know. I was surprised when Rebecca put her hand up. She seemed to know exactly how I was feeling. If she knew how it felt to be bullied, why was she bullying me?

When I went home that night I was brave and I talked about it to my sister. I told her everything, about how I felt and what was happening to me. She was great and came with me the next day to speak to my headteacher. Rebecca and I were both called to the office too. She broke down in tears. She said that she was bullied by her sister at home. It made me glad of my sister. I understood more about Rebecca's life and why she bullied me.

At the end of the story, say how the problem was sorted out.

The bullying has stopped now and I'm much happier at school. I wouldn't say Rebecca and I are the best of friends, but I think we have both learnt something about how bullying makes you feel.

Write the whole story as 'I' and say lots about how the bullying makes you feel.

CGP 2003

Mystery Stories

Good mystery stories don't tell you what's going on straightaway. You have to work it out, or wait until the end to find out. Make yours <u>hook</u> the reader, so they just <u>have</u> to finish the story.

RULES FOR A GREAT MYSTERY STORY...
- *Start with something unusual or dramatic to set the scene*
- *Give the reader clues to what has happened to build the suspense*
- *Add drama by making the main character ask questions*
- *Include mysterious sounds, lights or smells to add suspense*
- *Sometimes try putting a twist at the end, to surprise the reader*

Here's a SAT-style <u>mystery story</u> question...

> As Jimmy turned the corner and began walking towards his house, the sight that greeted him stopped him in his tracks. He could see broken glass and lots of blood...
>
> **Finish this mystery story.**
> **You do not need to re-write the first two sentences.**
>
> You will need to decide:
> - The ending first, so you can plan how you will build suspense
> - What clues to use to build the suspense
> - Whether to add a twist at the end

Plan your story before you write it.

What does Jimmy **think** has happened?
He thinks his house is being burgled.

What clues are there to make him think this?
Broken glass, blood on the floor and walls, missing TV and DVD player.

Think of clues that will really make the readers want to know what's going on.

Is there a **twist** at the end? What is it?
Yes — Dad took the TV and DVD player to the repair shop but locked himself out. He broke the side window but cut his hand. He is upstairs washing himself when Jimmy comes in.

You've got to decide the ending <u>before</u> you start wr so you can shape the sto towards the ending.

© CGP 200

Mystery Stories

Now you can use your plan to write a cracking mystery story. Choose the clues you give carefully, so that they build up suspense and keep readers hanging on your every word.

He ran towards his front door. A small window had been broken and there was a puddle of blood on the floor.

> Start describing the mystery from the very beginning.

"I knew it!" he thought to himself. There had been lots of break-ins over the past few weeks and it looked like his house had been targeted next.

He quietly lifted his mobile phone out of his pocket and called the police. He switched his phone off and unlocked the door, being careful not to touch the blood that was smeared on the side. As he entered the house, he could see that the television and DVD were missing.

> Put lots of clues in, so the readers *think* they know what's going on.

"I knew that we'd been burgled!" He suddenly froze at the sound of a tap running upstairs.

> Use strange sounds to add to the mystery.

"I don't believe it — I think they're still here!" he thought to himself. He curled his hand around the poker from the fire and bravely began to tiptoe towards the stairs. The tap abruptly stopped. Heavy footsteps began to move towards the door. He gripped his poker tighter and continued his slow walk up the narrow staircase.

> Give the story away a little bit at a time.

As he reached the top, he heard police sirens behind him. He rushed into the bathroom but the shock of what he saw stopped him in his tracks.

There in front of him was his Dad with a towel wrapped round his hand and blood stains all around the sink.

"Dad? What are you doing here?" asked Jimmy, his heart slowing down.

"Well, when I got back from the TV repair shop after dropping off the TV and DVD player, I realised I'd locked myself out," he explained. "I thought I could break in and fix it before anyone got back, but it all went wrong when I cut my hand!"

"But I thought you were a... I've called the police and everything... I was going to hit you with this..." stuttered Jimmy in total disbelief.

Dad laughed. "Never mind son, help me fix this window and explain to the police before your mum gets home, or it will be more than a cut hand that I'll have to worry about!"

> Make sure everything's explained by the end of the story.

Conversations

*Conversations keep a story moving and tell the reader
loads about the characters who are speaking.*

RULES FOR A GREAT CONVERSATION...

- *Use all the right punctuation — especially speech marks*
- *Each time a new person speaks, put their speech on a new line*
- *Use interesting verbs — think of other words to use instead of 'said'*
- *Just have two or three people speaking — if you have more it gets confusing*

Here's a SAT-style question for a __story with conversations__...

As the day drew on, the fog came down. It got thicker, until Sam and Navinder could barely see their hands in front of their faces. They were lost in the park!

"I can hardly see my hands, Sam." said Navinder nervously.
"Where are you Navinder?" replied Sam, "You sound miles away."
"I thought I was by your side! Oh no! We're lost!" shrieked Navinder.

Finish the story using conversations between the characters to help you.

You need to consider:
- What the characters decide to do
- How they get out of the situation

You don't need to tell the whole story with conversations — just bits of it.

Make a plan before you write your story.

How do Sam and Navinder **find** each other?

Sam stays still and talks loudly. Navinder walks towards his voice.

How do Sam and Navinder **get out** of the park?

They stop and listen out for the traffic on the road so they know which way to walk.

How does the story **end**?

Sam and Navinder make it to the gates of the park. They're happy and relieved.

© CGP 200.

Conversations

Put together all the ideas from your plan to produce a thrilling story with lots of conversation.
Make your conversations move the plot along and show how the characters are feeling.

Try not to use "said" at all if you can help it.

The cold fog surrounded the two children as they begin to panic. The trees were silent, the air was silent. No aeroplanes flew overhead, no birds were singing. The world had become silent, spooky and white.

"Sam, Sam, where are you?" shouted Navinder. → *Always put speech marks round the spoken words.*

Sam could hear the fear in her voice.

"It's alright, Navinder, I can hear you." Sam called with confidence. "I'm going to stand completely still and shout at the top of my voice. You must walk towards the sound and you'll find me."

"But what if I don't?" she called back into the empty whiteness.

"You will," bellowed Sam. "Are you ready?" ← *Start a new line when a new person speaks.*

He shouted at the top of his voice. Navinder followed the sound of his voice and was standing right next to him before she knew it.

"Well done Navinder," said Sam, "now all we've got to do is find our way out of here."

The two children stood for a moment and thought about how to get out. As they stood in silence, Navinder had an idea.

"Listen, can you hear the cars?" she asked excitedly.

"Of course I can. What about them?" asked Sam, sounding confused.

"Well that must mean the road is nearby and that's where the park gates are." She went on, "All we have to do is walk towards the sound of the cars."

The children began to make slow, careful steps towards the sound of the cars, stopping occasionally to make sure that the sounds were getting closer, not further away.

"Look!" shouted Sam, "I think I can see the pelican crossing flashing!"

The two children faced towards the road noises and began to feel much better straight away. They were relieved to see car headlights and the outline of the park gates.

"Miss Smith says that I talk too much and that I never listen!" smiled Sam. "I can't wait to see her tomorrow and tell her all about this!"

Use conversation to move the story on and show how the characters feel.

Historical Stories

A historical story is always set in the past. The characters and objects must match the time
that the story is set in — you couldn't put a digital watch into a story about Ancient Egypt!

RULES FOR A GREAT HISTORICAL STORY...

- Historical stories are basically adventure stories based on fact
- Use facts from history to make the story sound realistic
- Give the characters a mission, or send them on a difficult journey
- Make the characters talk and act like people did at that time in history

Here's a SAT-style _historical story_ question...

Germany, 9 March 1943, World War Two

Sergeant Wright and B company find themselves deep behind enemy
lines. Their mission is to overthrow the prisoner of war camp and
capture Herr Hamler, the cruel Nazi general.

Tell the story of B Company's mission, using as many facts as possible.
You need to decide:

- How the soldiers are feeling
- What happens when the soldiers attack
- What facts to use to make the story interesting and realistic

Always work out what your story is going to be about _before_ you start writing.

Who are the main characters?

_Sergeant Wright, Herr Hamler and
Foot Soldier Tremain._

How do the soldiers **feel** before attacking?

_Nervous, frightened,
determined, proud._

If you're not sure about the
facts, think about stories you've
read, or films you've seen.

What happens to add **action** to your story?

_The surprise attack starts with
lots of explosions and gunfire.
The sub-plot involves one soldier
whose brother is in the camp.
He is determined to free him._

What facts will you include about **WW2**?

_Captured soldiers were kept in tough
conditions in prisoner of war camps.
Weapons included machine guns,
grenades and tanks. Britain won the
war but lost a lot of soldiers._

Just because it's about the old days it doesn't
have to be boring. Make it as exciting as you can.

© CGP 2003

Historical Stories

Once you've got your ideas together, you can write a humdinger of a historical story. You've got to make the story exciting and include facts to make the story seem realistic.

The night was deadly black as the soldiers waited for the command from Sergeant Wright. As they lay in their green camouflage uniforms, with their faces blacked out, their nerves were alight with the thought of fighting. Their cue to attack was a short, sharp blow on the sergeant's whistle. Time seemed to stop as they waited in the darkness.

The whistle screeched and B Company surged forward towards the Nazi camp with machine guns blasting. The thick darkness was lit up by the flashes that came from the end of the guns.

> *Only mention weapons that really <u>were</u> used in the Second World War.*

"Take that!" yelled Tremain, as he tossed his grenade with anger and excitement.

He couldn't wait to get into the camp and find his brother who had been shot down over Berlin in his Lancaster Bomber.

> *Include details like the names of planes to make the story more convincing.*

"I'm coming to get you Billy," he roared over the gunfire, "Don't worry, big brother is here!"

Herr Hamler had been taken by surprise. His Nazi soldiers were not ready for the attack and were suffering heavy losses. As B Company poured into the camp, he knew he was surrounded but he continued to fire his pistol anyway. As he aimed, he saw Tremain throw a grenade at his hut. He saw the bomb fly through the air towards him and explode into a yellow and orange flash in front of him. He felt himself being flung through the air. He did not get up again.

> *Use short sentences to make things sound exciting.*

The night fell silent again and the soldiers knew the battle had been won. Tremain found his brother.

"What have they done to you, old man?" he gasped, as his thin, weary brother emerged from the shadows.

> *If you use slang, make it old-fashioned.*

"Whatever they've done to me, they won't be able to do again," he replied, "Thank you for coming, I knew you wouldn't forget."

As the two brothers hugged, the German soldiers were put into the cells.

"We may have won the battle but we haven't won the war," whispered Sergeant Wright, "so we will just have to keep on fighting to the very end, whenever it may come!"

Science Fiction Stories

A science fiction story is an adventure story set in a futuristic world, maybe in space or on a different planet. Usually science fiction stories involve a quest and lots of fancy gadgets.

RULES FOR A GREAT SCIENCE FICTION STORY...
- Set your story in space or in the future
- Write about a group of friends on a journey — as if it's an adventure story
- Include unusual species from different planets
- Include unbelievable settings and hi-tech gadgets and machines

---

Here's a SAT-style _science fiction story_ question...

> The year is 2134 and the Intergalactic Space Police are on the trail of a master criminal, who has stolen the Life Diamond (the diamond at the centre of the Earth that controls the planet's temperature).
>
> **Write a science fiction adventure based on this idea.**
> You will need to decide:
> - Who goes on the quest for the diamond
> - What fantasy gadgets they have
> - What problems they face on their journey and how they overcome them
> - How the quest ends

If you get a writing frame, use it to get your ideas straight before you start.

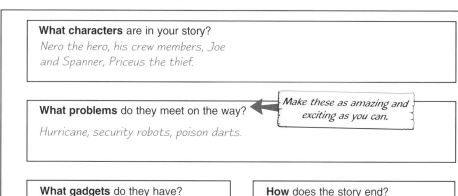

What characters are in your story?
Nero the hero, his crew members, Joe and Spanner, Priceus the thief.

What problems do they meet on the way?
Make these as amazing and exciting as you can.
Hurricane, security robots, poison darts.

What gadgets do they have?
Dust-guns, anti-illness ray.
Think of gadgets that fit in with your story.

How does the story end?
They get the diamond but Priceus escapes.

© CGP 2003

Science Fiction Stories

Turn your ideas into a stupendous science fiction story. Focus on the quest and the problems that turn up along the way — and stick in some fancy gadgets for added spice.

Show the readers they're in a different world right at the start.

With a galactic hurricane raging around him, Nero angled the space craft towards the entrance to Priceus' forest lair and landed with a bump. He turned to face his crew.

"We're here and there is no going back," he said in a confident voice. "Set your dust-guns to pulverise and lets move," he continued.

"Boss, look out!" exploded Spanner, but before Nero could even turn, ten metallic, mechanical poison darts had smashed through the windscreen and embedded themselves in his back.

Give the main characters dramatic problems to deal with.

Nero fell to the floor as the poison from the darts fired by Priceus' security robots began to flow into his bloodstream.

Spanner and Joe fired their dust-guns through the broken window and watched as the security robots turned to dust. More darts were flying through the gaping hole.

"The anti-illness ray!" screamed Joe. "Where is it?"

Joe fired his dust-gun at the approaching security robots as Spanner hurtled across the ship floor to find the anti-illness ray. He threw it to Joe, who aimed the ray at Nero and fired.

Make the gadgets an important part of the story.

A sky-blue laser covered Nero from head to toe, and the poison in his veins began to disappear through his skin. As the ray stopped, Nero awoke and stood up just in time to see the final security robot fall to the ground in a pile of dust.

The team ran through the forest and straight into the lair, taking the security robots by surprise. They burst through the electronic doors and grabbed Priceus.

"Where is it, Priceus?" screamed Nero. "I've got so many dust-guns pointing at you that they could turn your dust to dust!"

"I don't know what you mean." the villain replied. "This is an outrage!"

Whilst he was struggling, Spanner noticed the end of a bag protruding from the criminal's jacket. He grabbed it and the Life Diamond clattered to the floor. In a flash Nero grabbed it, but loosened his grip on Priceus. Priceus struggled free and lurched towards a door in the floor.

Give all the characters strange names.

"You may have the diamond, Nero, but I will return!" he said as he disappeared. The door locked tight behind him.

© CGP 2003

Humorous Stories

A humorous story should make your readers laugh until their bellies hurt.

RULES FOR A GREAT HUMOROUS STORY...

- *Have funny characters and make sure you describe them really well*
- *Include a boring character who makes the funny characters seem even funnier*
- *Turn normal, familiar situations into funny, odd situations*
- *Use conversations and detailed descriptions to make the readers chuckle*

Here's a SAT-style <u>humorous story</u> question...

"What time do you call this and where have you been?" screamed Tom's mum, as he scuttled through the door with a fish in one hand and a party hat on his head.

"Well, it all started when I bumped into Barry on my way to the chip shop…"

Finish off Tom's story using descriptions and conversations.

You will need to decide:
- Who Barry is, what he looks like and why he is so funny
- Why Tom is so late
- Other characters who are involved

Plan your story before you write it.

> *Make the characters believable by going into lots of detail.*

What does **Barry** look like?
Barry is a large boy — his clothes are always a bit too small. He has loads of messy, blond hair that's always in his eyes. Clumsy. Always has hair-brained ideas that usually get him and whoever is with him into trouble.

Why is Tom so **late** back home?
Barry suggests they try and catch their own fish to go with the chips to save some money. They borrow fishing gear and end up falling into the river and being chased by angry fishermen through town.

Who else is in the story?
Fishermen, people at a party.

> *Start out with a normal situation and make it get more and more ridiculous.*

How did Tom end up with a **fish** and a **party hat**?
The fish was in his pocket from the river and the hat came from a party that they ran through when they were escaping from the angry fishermen.

Humorous Stories

Once you've done a plan, you can write a rib-tickling humorous story.
The humour mainly comes from the funny characters and the
situations you put them in — be as silly as you like.

Start with an ~~ordinary~~ dinary situation.

Tom skipped out of the house, clutching the twenty-pound note that his mum had given him. He was on his way to the chip shop to buy tea when he bumped into his best friend, Barry.

Barry was tall for a twelve year old and his trousers never covered his ankles. Today he was wearing one Aston Villa sock and one Man United sock. He had a crop of blond hair that always draped over his eyes like curtains. Barry was clumsy and would often find himself flat on his face. His blue eyes sparkled with mischief.

Describe your funny character.

Liven up the story with conversations.

"What you up to Tom?" Barry asked, as he tripped up the kerb.
"I'm off to the chippy, fancy coming along?" Tom enquired.
"I've got a much better idea than that!" he said and made his way off to the reservoir. Tom followed.

Turn the normal situation into a more ridiculous one.

"The way I see it, Tom, we could save at least half of the twenty pounds by catching our own fish and cooking them ourselves. What do you think?" But before Tom had time to answer, Barry had borrowed a range of fishing equipment from a hut nearby and was crashing around, trying to put on a pair of long Wellington boots.

Describe slapstick movements to give readers a funny picture in their minds.

In a matter of minutes he had knocked over the entire hut and was splashing about in the water, with Tom trying to remove the Wellington boot that was stuck on his foot.

They didn't notice the string of angry fishermen that were running towards them until it was almost too late. Pulling themselves out of the water, they ran as fast as they could up the path to the road, with the fishermen close behind them.

At the end of the road was a pub with music blaring and people dancing.

"In here!" yelled Barry, and the two friends disappeared through the doors and joined in the party. Tom put party hats on their heads to disguise them both, and when the angry fishermen arrived they couldn't see the two boys at all, only the puddles that they had left on the ground. Disappointed and hot after the run, but much to Tom and Barry's delight, the fishermen decided to get a drink and join in the party as well.

Build up the story, so the silliest bits are at the end.

Very sneakily the boys slipped out by the back door and began running home with wet party hats on their heads, a raw fish in Tom's pocket and no fish and chips for their supper.

© CGP 2003

Stories With A Dilemma

A dilemma is a situation where you don't know what to do. A story with a dilemma makes the readers think about what they would do if they were stuck in a similar situation.

RULES FOR A GREAT DILEMMA STORY...

- *Introduce the main character first, then the dilemma*
- *Have an innocent central character or characters*
- *Choose a dilemma that readers will have experienced or heard about*
- *In your story explain how the main character solved the dilemma*
- *Write a moral ending that makes readers think*

Here's a SAT-style question for a <u>story with a dilemma</u>...

> Jenny and her friends face a problem. The Lard Street Gang have called them soft because they won't smoke cigarettes. Jenny doesn't want to lose face with her friends but she doesn't want to start smoking either.
>
> **Write a story about what Jenny decides to do.**
>
> You need to think about:
> - Where the drama takes place
> - How Jenny deals with the dilemma
> - A good ending that will make the reader think about how they would react

Make a plan before you write your story.

Where does the dare take place?

At the very end of the school fields where teachers can't see.

> *Set your dilemma in an everyday setting like a school.*

Who else is in the story?

Marcie, the leader of the Lard Street gang.
Jenny's friends. Jenny doesn't want to look soft in front of them.

> *Think about how the other characters will make Jenny feel.*

What does Jenny **choose** to do?

She takes the dare and smokes the cigarette.

What is the story **teaching** the reader?

You have to stand up to bullies to stop them picking on you.

> *Put the moral at the end of your story to make readers think about what they would do.*

© CGP 2003

Stories With A Dilemma

Now you can use your ideas to produce an impressive dilemma story.
In your story say what the dilemma is and how your main character deals with it.

> **Start with a quick introduction to the main character.**

Most people at Burton Street Primary liked Jenny, but the Lard Street Gang couldn't stand her. They were always picking on Jenny and teasing her.

One day the Lard Street Gang kept going on and on about smoking, saying Jenny was too scared to try it. Jenny knew smoking was stupid, but she didn't bother to explain. She just said, "OK, see you at the end of the field after school and I'll show you who's scared."

> **Introduce the dilemma early on.**
> **Jenny's dilemma is whether or not to smoke.**

At four o'clock, the girls formed a circle around Jenny on the playing field as she put the cigarette into her mouth.

"What's wrong Jenny, are you scared to go through with it?" sneered Marcie. The Lard Street Gang sniggered behind Marcie. They didn't particularly like Marcie. They were just glad that it wasn't them that she was picking on.

Jenny lit the cigarette. The end glowed fiery red and Jenny felt a fierce burning at the back of her throat as the smoke hit it. The taste was bad enough but the pain from the burning smoke was almost unbearable.

> **Tell the readers how the dilemma makes the main character feel.**

Jenny didn't show this at all. She knew that if she was going to keep face with both her friends and the gang she could show no fear.

"I don't see what all the fuss is about Marcie," she said trying to fight back the tears. "If this is supposed to make you look hard, surely it should be a little bit harder to handle than this!"

Some of the Lard Street Gang began to giggle. This gave Jenny the confidence she needed to carry on.

> **Show how the main character solves the dilemma.**

"I mean, come on Marcie, you could have given me something more difficult to show how uncool you are!" Jenny snorted.

All the girls in the circle were giggling and laughing at Marcie now who was going redder and redder. Jenny flicked the cigarette end on to the floor, put it out with her foot and walked off down the field, back to school. Everyone except Marcie followed her, laughing and cheering and asking her what it tasted like.

> **End by summing up the main character's thoughts.**

"It was revolting and it kills you and I'll never do it again," she replied, "but sometimes you've got to stand up to bullies or they never leave you alone."

© CGP 2003

Stories With A Twist

A story with a twist is meant to give the reader a massive surprise at the end of the story — the best twists are totally unexpected.

RULES FOR A GREAT STORY WITH A TWIST...

- *Put twists at the end of mystery stories*
- *Put clues in the story to make readers expect one ending*
- *In your twist make the clues add up to a different ending*
- *Save the twist for the very end of your story*

Here's a SAT-style question for a <u>story with a twist</u>...

Ben could hear a noise. It was coming from his cellar.
He decided to investigate.

What does Ben find in the cellar? Tell the story of his investigation, but try to add a twist at the end.

You will need to decide:

- How to build up suspense
- What is making the noise
- What the twist in your story is

Always work out what your story is going to be about <u>before</u> you start writing.

What does Ben **think** is making the noise?

A blood-curdling child-eating monster with razor-sharp claws and sharp brown teeth.

Make the thing Ben imagines sound really bad.

What is making the noise?

A dog.

What is the **twist** at the end?

The blood-curdling child-eating monster is also in the cellar, and it's eaten the dog that was down there.

The twist should be a complete surprise.

© CGP 2003

Stories With A Twist

Use your plan to write a cracking story with a twist. You need to build suspense and trick the reader into thinking everything is OK, until you unleash your devilish twist.

Scratch, scratch, scratch. ← **Start with something really spooky to make your readers nervous.**

Ben woke up. He opened up his curtains to look outside. Moonlight spilled into his room. He was listening. He wanted to hear the sound again, the sound that had woken him up. He opened the window and it became clear that the sound was coming from somewhere below him.

Ben picked up his torch and began to creep downstairs. His mind was filled by the images of monsters with razor-sharp claws and sharp brown teeth. Why was he even going to look? ← **Hint at what's going to happen, but don't give too much away.**

Scratch, scratch, scratch.

He thought about the ugliest, scariest, meanest monsters he could think of. He imagined that there were blood-curdling, child-eating monsters, who were hiding in his cellar to eat him alive. He wondered if he would have time to scream or fight or run. He was at the bottom of the stairs when he heard it again.

Scratch, scratch, scratch.

The sound was louder now and Ben could tell that it was coming from the cellar. He walked towards the door, picking up a broom from the kitchen as he passed.

Scratch, scratch, scratch.

Ben opened the basement door. The darkness was suffocating. The light no longer worked, so Ben shone his torch into the darkness and searched the basement floor. He began to walk down the stairs one by one. As he got further down the stairs, he heard it again. He turned to face the noise and saw a dog collar lying on the floor. Breathing a sigh of relief, he walked towards it to find its owner.

Make the clues add up to something that seems OK — the readers will think Ben's going to find a dog.

As he looked at the collar, Ben noticed that it was covered in blood, and he realised with horror that it was all that was left of the dog, eaten by the blood-curdling monster. The sound came again, closer than ever and he knew that his worst nightmares had come true...

Save the twist till last. It's not a dog. It really is a blood-curdling monster...

© CGP 2003

NON-FICTION WRITING

Factual Reports

A good factual report sticks to telling important facts and does it clearly and concisely.
The language is fairly formal and there usually aren't any descriptions.

RULES FOR A GREAT FACTUAL REPORT...

- Tell the reader when and where the event took place
- Write about the important facts — don't include irrelevant details
- Tell the events in the order that they happened
- Use formal language that's clear and to-the-point
- Don't include lots of long descriptions
- Finish with a conclusion

Here's a SAT-style <u>factual report</u> question...

> Your class has just been taken on a trip to the zoo to learn about wild animals.
>
> **Write a factual report about your class day out at the zoo.**
>
> You will need to decide:
>
> - When and where you went
> - What important things you saw and did there
> - What the class learnt

Plan your report out before you write it.

> *Get the events in order here.*

When and **where** did the class go to visit the zoo?

Tuesday 4th March, 2003,
at Wycroft Zoo

What important things did you **do** and **see** there?

1. Looked at different kinds of animals.
2. Had a talk from a zoo guide — we took notes and did sketches.
3. Group discussion about what we learnt.

What did the class **learn**?

What kinds of animals live in water,
how humans are related to apes, how
animals are adapted to living in
different continents

What is the **conclusion**?

It was a good day out, and we all
learnt a lot about the animals.

> *Make sure all the facts in the report are relevant*
> *— only give the important information.*

Factual Reports

Now put together the ideas from your writing grid and write an accurate factual report.

Keep the language formal all the way through.

Tell the reader what the report's about in the very first sentence.

On Tuesday 4th March, 2003, my class (class 7) from Pepton Primary School visited Wycroft Zoo in the Midlands.

The reason for the trip was that we had been studying wild animals in class and our teacher, Mrs Hamil, thought that the best way for us to learn would be to see the animals in the flesh.

We set off at 9am and reached the zoo mid-morning. First of all we visited the aquarium. Inside were many interesting species of fish, and we learnt that there are some mammals that live in the water too, such as whales and otters.

The report writes about events in the order that they happened.

Secondly, we went to look at the monkeys and apes. A zoo guide gave us a talk on how we are related to apes. We took photographs, drew sketches and wrote notes so that we could do a presentation on humans and apes when we got back to school.

In the afternoon we split into groups, and each group went to look at a animals from a different continent. My group was looking at wild animals from Africa. We saw loads of different animals, including lions, leopards, elephants and giraffes.

At 4pm, just before we had to leave, all the groups got together and we all compared the different animals we had seen. Mrs Hamil told us particularly to notice how the animals are adapted to living in their continent. We noticed that a lot of the African animals have special ways of keeping cool — for example the elephants have big ears that they flap to cool themselves down.

We left the zoo at 4:45pm and travelled back to school by bus, where we were met by our parents.

You don't need to say what songs you sang on the bus — just give the important facts.

It was a really good day out at the zoo. We all learnt a lot about wild animals and have gathered a lot of information that we can use to do a really interesting presentation at school. Mrs Hamil was right — the best way to learn about things is to see them up close.

Finish off with a conclusion — don't just tail off.

Factual Reports

Letters to Friends and Family

Letters to people you know should be written in a <u>friendly</u>, <u>informal</u> way.
You'll usually be telling them about something interesting that's happened recently.

RULES FOR A GREAT LETTER TO FRIENDS OR FAMILY...

- *Write your address and the date in the top right hand corner*
- *Start your letter with 'Dear ...' and use their first name*
- *Use your first sentence to ask how they are and give the reason for your letter*
- *Write about what you've been doing — about three paragraphs should do it*
- *End your letter with a friendly comment, like 'Lots of love', and your first name*

Here's a SAT-style <u>informal letter</u> question...

> Imagine you have just got back from a foreign holiday.
>
> **Write a letter to your Grandma that tells her all about it.**
>
> You will need to think about:
>
> - Where you have been
> - The three most exciting things that happened while you were there
> - Who you went with
> - How you are going to begin and end your letter

Make a plan before you write the letter.

> *Start and end letters to people you know in a friendly way.*

How will you **start** the letter? *I hope you are well. I've just got back from Spain and I wanted to tell you all about it.*

> **What three things** are you going to tell Grandma about?
> *Arriving at the hotel and thinking the rooms were mixed up*
> *My brother falling into the pool*
> *Waiting at the airport when the plane was late*

> **Who** was with you on holiday?
> *Mum, Dad, brother*

How will you **end** the letter? *I hope I can come and see you soon to show you the photographs. All my love.*

                    © CGP 2003

Letters to Friends and Family

Now you've got some ideas about writing your informal letter, you should be able to get started. You've probably written stacks of them before and never really thought about it.

33, Cherry Tree Close
Middlebrook
Nottinghamshire
NO2 5YJ
28.05.03

Put the address and date at the top of the right-hand side.

Start off with "Dear".

Dear Grandma,

Explain what the main point of your letter is.

I hope you are well, I've just got back from Spain and I wanted to tell you all about it. We arrived at Madrid airport at 7.30pm, but by the time we had got through the airport, had something to eat and travelled to our hotel, it was 10.30pm. We were all very tired and couldn't wait just to fall into bed. I'm sure you can imagine our surprise then, when the hotel porter opened the room door and showed us into a room with only one single bed! Dad hit the roof, until the porter opened a door in the wall that we thought was a wardrobe. It opened up into a second room with three more beds, thank goodness!

Write about things the person reading would want to know.

The hotel was lovely and the pool was great. Charlie thought it was terrific until he fell in it accidentally. We were making our way down to the restaurant at night, for our favourite, chicken and chips, when Charlie thought he would walk by the side of the pool. None of us noticed until we heard a mighty splash and saw his sombrero floating on top of the water! Mum was furious and had to take him upstairs to get changed again!

We didn't want to leave as we made our way to the airport on our way home. That soon changed when we were told that our plane was late and that we would be waiting for 5 hours! Mum tried to keep us all entertained, but it was really boring, especially when we knew what fun we could be having back at the hotel. Eventually we boarded the plane and arrived back home at 2 o'clock in the morning, tired but glad to be home.

I hope I can come and see you soon to show you the photographs.

All my love,

Ellen

End in a warm, friendly way. Things like "Yours sincerely," are only for formal letters.

Don't use any formal language. Write exactly as though you were talking to your Gran.

Formal Letters

Formal letters are letters that you write to people you <u>don't know</u>.
You'll usually be writing to ask for advice, complain about something or give information.

RULES FOR A GREAT FORMAL LETTER...

- Write your address in the top right-hand corner with the date two lines underneath
- Use formal English
- Say clearly why you are writing the letter in your opening sentence
- Start a new paragraph for each new point you make
- If you don't know the name of the person you're writing to, start your letter with 'Dear Sir or Madam,' and end with 'Yours faithfully,'
- If you do know their name, start 'Dear ....,' and end with 'Yours sincerely,'

Here's a SAT-style <u>formal letter</u> question...

> The local council is planning to build a new shopping arcade on your local park, but it needs to know the opinions of local people. The swings, pond and football pitches will be replaced with new shops, a cinema and a large car park.
>
> **Write a formal letter to your local council saying whether you agree or disagree with the plans.**
>
> You will need to consider:
>
> - Who will be affected by the plans
> - Who will benefit from the plans and who will lose out
> - Whether the whole community will benefit or lose out

Always work out what you want to say <u>before</u> you start writing.

How will you **begin** your letter? *I am writing to complain about the council's plans to build a shopping arcade on Greenspace Park.*

Who will be **affected** by the plans?
joggers, dog walkers, children, footballers

Who will be **lose out** because of the plans?
local hospice and fun-runners

Do you think the plans are a good idea overall?
no — the community will lose out

How will you **end** your letter? *Thank you for taking the time to read my letter and I hope you take my views into consideration before you make your decision.*

© CGP 2003

Formal Letters

Now you've got some ideas about your letter, you can get it written.
Remember to use formal language and make the things you want to say clear and precise.

26 Spectacle Avenue
Reading
Berkshire
ICU 4AT

20.02.03

Start your letter like this if you don't know the name of the person you're writing to.

Put your address and the date at the top of the right-hand side.

Dear Sir or Madam,

I am writing to complain about the council's plans to build a shopping arcade on Greenspace Park.

Tell the reader why you're writing in the first sentence.

The park is the only piece of green land for our community and is used every day by joggers, dog walkers, children and families. It is the only place for our local footballers to play safely and it hosts the annual charity fun run.

Every year the fun run raises thousands of pounds for the hospice. People enter the event because they enjoy running in the park and I fear that they wouldn't enter if they knew that they would have to run through the streets.

Start a new paragraph for each new point.

My final point is about the future of our community. The park is used throughout the year by children. The green space is perfect for football and the running track around the park is great for racing. The concrete path is used by skateboarders and cyclists. Children these days do not get enough exercise and so to take away a piece of land that children use regularly is only going to encourage them to play on the streets, which is dangerous, or to stay inside, which is unhealthy.

Thank you for taking the time to read my letter and I hope you take my views into consideration before you make your decision.

This letter ends like this because the writer doesn't know the person he is writing to.

Yours faithfully,

Harry Roy

Stick to formal language all the way through.

Adverts and Flyers

A good advert or flyer makes readers <u>really</u> want to buy the product being advertised.

RULES FOR A GREAT ADVERT OR FLYER...

- *Use exciting and attention-grabbing words and phrases*
- *Use an interesting layout and clear, bold writing to grab readers' attention*
- *Make the reader believe they couldn't live without the product*
- *Use clear language so the reader understands what you are selling*

Here's a SAT-style <u>flyer</u> question...

Stink-Go soap company are bringing out a new type of soap, designed for children.

**Design a flyer for the new soap,
that will make children really want to buy it.**

You will need to decide:

- What is special about the soap
- How you'll make children want to buy it
- How to lay out the flyer

If you're given a writing frame, use it to get your ideas straight before you start.

What is the soap called?	**What's special** about the soap?
'Bubble-Trouble Soap' *Think of a really attention-grabbing name.*	*It bubbles up into giant bubbles that keep growing until they explode with a loud pop.*
How will you make children want to **buy** the soap?	**What else** will you need to put in the flyer?
Ask the readers lots of questions that make the soap seem really appealing. Make the bubbles sound like really good fun.	*How much the item is, how you use it and what else they have on sale.*

Put yourself in the reader's shoes — what would make <u>you</u> want to buy the product?

© CGP 2003

Adverts and Flyers

Turn your ideas into a fantastic, fabulous flyer advert.

ARE YOU SICK OF DULL SOAP THAT JUST DOESN'T MAKE WASHING FUN?

DO YOU OFTEN PRETEND YOU'VE WASHED, WHEN REALLY YOU HAVEN'T — BECAUSE IT'S JUST SOOOO BORING?

ARE YOU ALWAYS BEING NAGGED TO WASH BEHIND YOUR EARS?

IF THE ANSWER TO ALL THESE QUESTIONS IS YES, YOU NEED...

> *Use big writing for really important things like the product name.*

> *Ask the readers questions to make them think about the product.*

BUBBLE-TROUBLE SOAP!!!!!!

Yes, new from the Stink-Go soap company comes a great new product, BUBBLE-TROUBLE SOAP. It looks and acts just like a normal soap but just wait until you add water to it!!

As soon as it comes into contact with water, it starts foaming up into huge bubbles that just get bigger and bigger until they're almost the same size as you! When they reach maximum size they burst with a loud popping sound — great for scaring unsuspecting brothers and sisters!

So trips to the bathroom need no longer be boring — you'll be the envy of all your friends with this amazing soap. You'll love using it so much that your parents will never have to nag you to wash again — in fact they won't be able to keep you out of the bathroom!

> *Use catchy and exciting words and phrases to make the product sound more fun.*

FRIENDS WILL ENVY YOU!

PARENTS WILL STOP NAGGING YOU!

> *Write stuff you want people to notice on separate lines.*

BROTHERS AND SISTERS WILL RESPECT YOU!

Each wonderful bar is priced at a pocket-money affordable 75p, so don't delay — get bubbling today, with Stink-Go's BUBBLE-TROUBLE SOAP!!!

* ALSO, LOOK OUT FOR 'FOAM-ZONE' BUBBLE BATH — COMING SOON!!!

> *Use simple language — it should be easy for anyone to read.*

Diaries

A good diary should be an interesting <u>daily record</u> of events. They can be fiction or non-fiction, and they let the readers know about the writer's life and feelings.

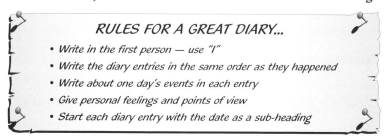

RULES FOR A GREAT DIARY...

* *Write in the first person — use "I"*
* *Write the diary entries in the same order as they happened*
* *Write about one day's events in each entry*
* *Give personal feelings and points of view*
* *Start each diary entry with the date as a sub-heading*

Here's a SAT-style <u>diary</u> question...

> **Write a diary that tells the story of an important time in your life.**
>
> You will need to decide:
>
> * How many days to include in your diary
> * Why this time in your life is important
> * How you feel about the event
> * How to express your emotions in the diary

Plan what you're going to say before you start writing your diary.

What event have you chosen to write about?	**How many** days will your diary last?
The build-up to the school cup final I was playing in.	*Three days.*

Just write about a few days so you can put plenty of detail on each day.

What is important about this event?	**What emotions** do you feel?
I was very nervous but I ended up scoring the winning goal.	*Nervousness, excitement, happiness*

Write about big emotions to make it interesting for the readers.

© CGP 2003

Diaries

Now you've planned your diary and you know what you need to make it great. Don't forget to describe your feelings in the diary.

<u>*Thursday 14th June 2002*</u> | *Start each day with a new heading.*

I couldn't believe it when I saw my name on the list of the football team that would be playing for the inter-school trophy. I'd been dreading going to school all day and when Bodie came running out to tell us that Mr Farrah had picked the team my belly sank into my socks. But I'm in the team for the most important match of the season and I'm playing in my favourite position — striker.

Football training was great tonight, everyone was buzzing. I told my mum and dad as soon as they got in from work and they phoned everyone in the family. They're all coming on Saturday, which will make me even more nervous.

| *Talk about how things made you feel — diaries are where people write down their personal thoughts and feelings.*

<u>*Friday 15th June 2002*</u>

I can't remember ever feeling more nervous or excited in my life. But I know that as soon as I run onto the pitch on Saturday, I will be fine because I will hear my friends and family on the sidelines. Today was a blur really because all I could think about was tomorrow. Mr Farrah wished us luck in assembly and all day people were coming up to us and doing the same. Mum cooked me a special good luck tea. I hope I sleep tonight!

| *When you get to the end of the day, finish the entry and start a new one.*

<u>*Saturday 16th June 2002*</u>

What a day and what a victory! One-all with two minutes to go and Bodie lifted the perfect cross over to me. Now I'm not saying my winning goal was goal of the season, but it was very good. I headed it into the top corner and the keeper didn't even see it. The crowd erupted as the whistle blew and I found myself hidden under my team mates and friends. I'm so happy and excited, I can't stop smiling. Like I said, what a day and what a victory!

Discussing Issues

*Issues are problems that people have different opinions about. Pieces of writing that discuss
issues should be about all the opinions, so that readers can make up their own minds.*

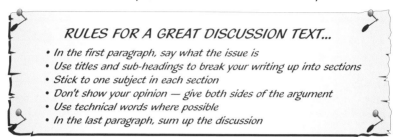

RULES FOR A GREAT DISCUSSION TEXT...

- *In the first paragraph, say what the issue is*
- *Use titles and sub-headings to break your writing up into sections*
- *Stick to one subject in each section*
- *Don't show your opinion — give both sides of the argument*
- *Use technical words where possible*
- *In the last paragraph, sum up the discussion*

Here's a SAT-style question asking you to __discuss issues__...

> Many people think that what children see on television and at the cinema affects
> how they behave in real life. They think programmes such as 'Eastenders' and
> films such as 'Lord of the Rings' should not be shown to children at all.
>
> **Write a balanced discussion for your school newspaper that takes
> both sides of the argument into consideration.**
>
> You will need to decide:
>
> - The types of programme shown on TV and the times they are shown
>
> - The types of film children watch and how children are protected at cinemas
>
> - The type of behaviour that might influence children

Make a plan before you start writing.

What types of **behaviour** are seen on the television and in films?
*Violence, swearing, smoking, drinking and drugs /
good, responsible, moral behaviour*

> Think about both sides of the
> argument for your plan.

How do TV and film companies stop children seeing things they shouldn't?
Do they work?
*Films have PG, 12 and 15 certificates but they don't stop kids seeing films.
TV companies give warnings but some kids allowed to watch anyway.*

Who is **responsible** for what children see on TV and at the cinema? *Television and
film companies, parents and children*

© CGP 2003

Discussing Issues

Now you can use your plan to write a great balanced argument.
Remember not to give away your own opinion.

> Introduce the issue in the first paragraph.

Many people think that children copy what they see on television and in films but others disagree and say there is no proof that this really happens.

> Put a sub-heading before each new point. It makes the discussion easier to read.

The Dangers

It is true that there is a lot of dangerous and violent behaviour on television and at the cinema. Many films and television programmes show fighting, wars, crime and drugs.

Some children could find these things interesting and try to copy them at school, for example by trying to fight like a superhero. Other children could get interested in drugs or smoking if they saw cool characters doing this on television.

The Benefits

Even if there are a lot of children who copy what they see on television, most children are not like that. Children could learn a lot from seeing films about crimes or drugs and avoid them in the future.

> Use technical terms if you know them. It sounds more convincing.

Protection for Children

It is not easy for children to see really violent films or programmes with very bad behaviour. Television companies wait till the 'watershed' at 9pm to show programmes with violence or bad language. If children try and see a film about drug-dealing or murders at the cinema, it will probably have a 15 or 18 certificate and they will not be allowed into the cinema.

Are Children Harming Themselves?

Even though there are regulations to protect children from seeing the wrong kinds of films and television programmes these might not be enough. Some people say that some soap operas and dramas are too realistic and could harm children. Children who really want to see a 15 or 18 film could watch it on video.

> Ask questions to make the readers think about the issue.

Who Is Responsible?

Some people say that the film companies and television companies should not make the more violent films at all. Others say that parents should decide what their children should be allowed to watch. You could also say that it is up to each child to think about what they watch and about whether it is a good idea to behave in the same way as the characters they see on television or on the cinema screen.

Discussing Issues

Writing About Your Point of View

Your point of view is your _opinion_ — when you write about your point of view
you're telling readers exactly how you feel about something.

RULES FOR WRITING ABOUT YOUR POINT OF VIEW...

- _Use a title that shows your point of view_
- _Say exactly what your point of view is in the first paragraph_
- _In each paragraph give a reason for your point of view_
- _Include facts and evidence to back up your reasons_
- _Use clear, concise, formal language_

Here's a SAT-style question asking you to _write about your point of view_...

Vegetarians don't like eating meat. Some don't eat it because they think it is
cruel whilst others just don't like the taste. Many meat eaters enjoy the flavour
of meat and say it is natural to eat it because we are carnivores.

Write about your opinion on eating meat.

You will need to decide:

- Whether you agree or disagree with eating meat, and why
- Whether you are stating your opinion or persuading people to agree with you
- The type of language to use

Always work out what you want to say before you start writing.

Do you agree or disagree with eating meat? _I strongly disagree with eating meat._

Three reasons for your point of view:

Back up your point
of view with reasons,
facts and evidence.

1. _Human beings are intelligent enough to choose a diet which doesn't
   harm other creatures._
2. _A vegetarian diet has been proved to be healthier than a meat diet.
   Meat diets are unhealthy because of the bad things that are fed to animals._
3. _Animals are kept in terrible conditions, with disease and overcrowding.
   Humans should stop eating meat so that this doesn't have to happen._

Are you **stating an opinion** or **persuading** the reader? _stating opinion_

What phrases will you use to show your point of view? _innocent animals /
modern vegetarian diets / cramped, cruel environments_

Writing About Your Point of View

Now you have planned you're your piece of writing, you should be able to knock the reader's socks off. By the time they've read it, they might even agree with you.

> Stick to formal language — it sounds more serious.

<u>Meat is Murder</u> ← Show your point of view in the title.

In my opinion, eating meat is wrong and killing innocent animals to feed human beings is cruel. ← Say exactly what your opinion is in the opening lines.

Some people say that human beings are natural carnivores and therefore need to eat meat. Carnivores have long canine teeth for tearing meat so surely it is what nature intended. I disagree with this because human beings are the most intelligent creatures on the planet — intelligent enough to make a choice and to decide whether it is cruel to kill animals in enormous numbers.

> Back up your points with solid facts.

Others say that a vegetarian diet is lacking in vital proteins and vitamins that you can only get from meat. I disagree with this point of view because modern vegetarian diets have been proven to contain a better balance of vitamins, minerals and proteins than a meat-eating diet. Animals are often force-fed to make sure they are fat and the things they eat are then eaten by the meat-eater, making it a very unhealthy diet.

Animals are forced to live in cramped, cruel environments. The farmers who keep them are only interested in the money they can get from their 'stock' and so conditions are not always clean or healthy. The recent outbreak of foot-and-mouth disease showed that diseases can break out in these environments very quickly.

> Don't make more than one point in each paragraph.

There are more vegetarians now than at any other time in history. In a modern twenty-first century world , I feel we should be able to make changes to our diet that show our understanding of a healthy diet and sympathy towards the animals that are forced to suffer for human need.

> Say what your point of view is again, at the end of the piece.

Writing an Argument

Good arguments are very clear and organised and include
lots of facts to make the argument more convincing.

RULES FOR A GREAT ARGUMENT...

- Start with a short introduction, saying what you think
- Stick to three or four main points, to keep your argument simple and strong
- Make your points in clear, simple sentences
- Don't just give your opinions — back them up with lots of convincing facts
- Sum up your argument at the end

Here's a SAT-style question asking you to _write an argument_...

> You read a quote in the newspaper that says:
>
> "All children are mindless idiots who watch too much television and have no idea how to behave. If I had my way they would all be put in the army, as it didn't do me any harm." (Mr D. Green)
>
> **Write a reply to the editor, arguing against the views in the letter.**
>
> You will need to decide:
>
> - What points you will make to argue against Mr. Green
> - What facts to include to back up your argument
>
> _The answer needs to be in letter format — look back at the Formal Letter rules on pages 36-37._

If you're given a writing frame, use it to get your ideas straight before you start.

What points will you make in your argument?

1. _Children are not "mindless idiots"_
2. _Children don't watch too much television_
3. _Children do know how to behave_

Always back up your points, otherwise nobody will believe you.

What points will you make to **back up** your argument?

1. _We are taught well and have a challenging curriculum. Will achieve L4 in all my SATs._
2. _Only watch television when there is something good on. Enjoy reading and music too._
3. _We are taught to be well-behaved and respectful of others in school and by parents._

How will you **end** your argument? _Politely but firmly_

© CGP 2003

Writing an Argument

When your plan's made, you can put down your argument.
Remember to back up your points to win readers over.

Dear Sir or Madam,

> *Start by making it clear what you think.*

I am writing in response to the quote you published from Mr D. Green. I strongly disagree with him and would like to put forward my argument against him.

> *Make a separate point in each paragraph.*

Firstly, Mr. Green suggested that all children are mindless idiots. This is a very unfair comment and ignores the many children such as myself who take great pride in school work and have worked very hard to achieve level 4 and 5 in our SATs. I thoroughly enjoy many different activities and I want to be a vet when I grow up. Many of my friends want to be solicitors, doctors and teachers. If we were mindless idiots we would never be able to achieve our goals.

> *Use words like "firstly" and "secondly" to make it obvious when you start a new point.*

> *Back up your points with evidence.*

Secondly, Mr. Green said that all children watch too much television. My friends and I only watch television when there is something worth watching such as Blue Peter or Art Attack. We prefer to read or go out on our bikes. I would rather be fit and healthy than a couch potato. I agree that some children watch too much television, but not all of us.

> *Use simple sentences to keep your argument clear.*

Finally, Mr. Green claimed that children don't know how to behave. Most children I know at school and at Guides are polite and respect adults. Mr Green has obviously only had experience of a small number of naughty children. Maybe they were rude to him or were acting silly. I agree that some children can be badly behaved, but at my school we all help them to change their ways by being patient.

It is a shame that Mr. Green's experiences of children have made him feel the way he does. I would like to meet him and show him that children aren't all bad. I am sure after meeting me and my friends, he would change his mind and not want to send us into the army.

> *Finish off in a friendly polite way — you want to convince the readers, not upset them.*

Yours faithfully,

Sophie Otterburn

Recounting Events

*'Recounting' means giving a true account of real events. Make your recounts
as accurate as possible, and include all the important details.*

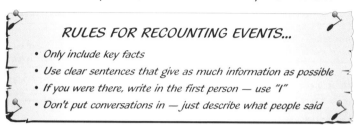

RULES FOR RECOUNTING EVENTS...

* *Only include key facts*
* *Use clear sentences that give as much information as possible*
* *If you were there, write in the first person — use "I"*
* *Don't put conversations in — just describe what people said*

Here's a SAT-style question asking you to recount events...

You have witnessed a handbag snatch on your local high street and the police
are interviewing witnesses to gather evidence.

**Recount the events to the police, making sure you include as many
important facts as you can, to help them catch the thief.**

You will need to include:

* Where and when the snatch took place

* What the thief looked like

* What happened next

Decide what to include in your recount before you write it.

Where did the snatch take place? *Outside the chip shop*

*Include lots of details to
make the report useful.*

What did the thief **look like**?

*He was about twenty-five and had long, blond hair underneath a red baseball cap.
He wore jeans, a black t-shirt, a grey hooded sweatshirt and black trainers.*

What did you see **happen**?

*The thief ran up to a woman standing outside the supermarket.
He grabbed her black bag and ran off into the crowd.*

What did you **do**?

I ran after him but lost him in the shopping centre.

*Make sure you write in the first
person — it's about what you saw.*

Recounting Events

Now you can use your plan to write an astounding account that includes key facts and clear descriptions. Remember to give as much detail as possible to the person reading your account.

Start with a date — it makes the account more official.

Wednesday 16th April, 2003

You don't need an introduction. Go straight into telling the facts.

I was walking down the High Street at about 12.30pm when I stopped to buy a chip butty at 'Bernie's Fish Bar'. I came out of the shop and sat on a nearby bench. All sorts of people were walking by but I wasn't really taking much notice until I saw a man running through the crowded streets. He caught my eye because he was the only person running, and when he ran up to a black-haired woman and grabbed her handbag, I started taking even more notice.

Write in simple sentences.

He was about twenty-five or twenty-six and was very thin. He had shoulder-length, blond hair and he was wearing a bright red baseball cap with a picture of an eagle on the front. He was wearing a black T-shirt underneath a light grey hooded sweatshirt. The sweatshirt had the words "New York City" on the front. He was wearing dark blue jeans and black Adidas trainers. His trainers had three white stripes down the side. He was alone.

The woman was standing outside the supermarket, talking to her friend. The man rushed up to her and without looking at her face, grabbed her black leather handbag. She didn't have time to hold onto the bag. The thief snatched it and turned around in a flash to set off the way he had come. She shouted for him to come back but he had gone.

Don't forget — use indirect speech. Describe what people said.

I dropped my chip butty and ran across the street after the thief. I almost caught hold of the hood on his sweatshirt but he was just too quick. He sped off into the shopping centre with the handbag under his arm and his head down.

Keep the language simple. You don't need fancy descriptions, feelings or ideas — just the facts.

Articles

Articles are the pieces of writing you find in magazines and newspapers.
They tell people about real facts and real events.

RULES FOR A GREAT ARTICLE...

• Cover all the important facts about the event or subject you're writing about
• Use exciting words to keep readers interested
• Present all the facts fairly and write about both sides of the argument
• Include quotes from people involved in the story
• Use your conclusion to sum up the facts and mention your own opinion

---

Here's a SAT-style <u>article</u> question...

Your school has just started a weekly newsletter and they need students to write articles for it.

Write an article for the school newsletter — it could be a sports article or an article about an event that has happened in school.

You will need to include:

• What event the article is about
• What facts to write about
• What quotes to include

Make a plan before you write the article.

What event are you writing about? *Teachers versus children football match*

What facts will you write about?

Who played well, who scored a goal, final score ◄ | *Make your article really detailed — it'll be more interesting to read.*

What quotes will you include? ◄ | *Put in quotes from people who were actually there, e.g. the players, or experts, e.g. a football commentator.*

Quotes from a teacher and a pupil who played in the game.

How will you **end** your article? *wondering whether the match will happen again*

© CGP 2003

Articles

Use your ideas from the grid to write the article.
Remember it has to tell all sides of the story, without any bias.

Start off with a headline that sums up the story.

FOOTBALL: TEACHERS NIL - PUPILS WON!

On Thursday, an unusual event took place on the school sports field — the school staff took on the school football team in a battle of 7-a-side football.

Say what the article's about in the first paragraph.

Before the kick-off, the staff definitely believed they would win the game. "I think it will be 6-0 to the staff," said Mr. Baxter, the year 3 teacher. Certainly, with dinner lady, Mrs. Flagstaff, in goal, the staff did seem to have an advantage.

Tell both sides of the story to make your article fair.

But they did not take into account the skill and superb footwork of the school team, most noticeably class 4's Natasha Johnstone and class 5's James Summerbee. The first ten minute half seemed to fly by, with most of the action happening around the staff's penalty area. Some fantastic saves from Mrs. Flagstaff kept the teachers in the game, and governor and referee, Mrs. Jones, blew the whistle for half time with the score at 0-0.

Quote from people on both sides.

"I think that their age is beginning to show," said school team goal-keeper, Josie Forlawn. That appeared to be the truth as Mrs. Townsend said, "I'm sure there are more than 7 of them, they seem to be everywhere!"

Use descriptive words to make your article more colourful.

The second half kicked-off, and Year 6 John Simmons charged up the pitch avoiding two staff defenders and crossing the ball neatly across the box towards Natasha Johnstone's head. However, the ball was intercepted by the hand of Mr. Baxter!

Mrs Jones could make no other decision than a penalty.

James Summerbee placed the ball on the spot and had no trouble in putting it to the right-hand side of Mrs. Flagstaff. The final whistle blew and the score was 1-0 to the school team — the teachers had been beaten!

"That was fantastic, we should do it every year!" said team captain, Christopher Woodward. The teachers appeared to agree but, judging from their tired faces and wobbly legs, they would find it hard to cope with a re-match — it might just finish them off!

In the last paragraph, sum up the story. If you want to say what you think about the story, do it here.

Biographies

A biography is a factual account of someone else's life. Biographies are often about famous people, but can be written about anyone you know — even an animal...

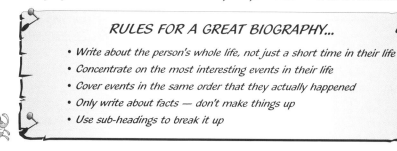

RULES FOR A GREAT BIOGRAPHY...

- *Write about the person's whole life, not just a short time in their life*
- *Concentrate on the most interesting events in their life*
- *Cover events in the same order that they actually happened*
- *Only write about facts — don't make things up*
- *Use sub-headings to break it up*

Here's a SAT-style biography question...

> **Write a biography about the achievements of someone (person or animal) close to you.**
>
> You will need to decide:
> - Who you are writing about
> - What they have achieved
> - How to make it interesting to read
> - How to finish the biography

Always work out what you want to say before you start writing.

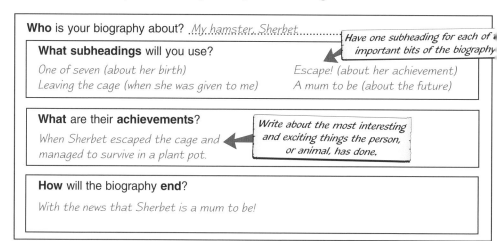

Who is your biography about? *My hamster, Sherbet*

Have one subheading for each of important bits of the biography

What subheadings will you use?

One of seven (about her birth)
Leaving the cage (when she was given to me)
Escape! (about her achievement)
A mum to be (about the future)

What are their **achievements**?

When Sherbet escaped the cage and managed to survive in a plant pot.

Write about the most interesting and exciting things the person, or animal, has done.

How will the biography **end**?

With the news that Sherbet is a mum to be!

© CGP 2003

Biographies

Use the ideas that you put together in your plan and try to use all of the rules.
That way you'll end up with something like this...

...y who the biography's about in the title. →

THE LIFE OF SHERBET, THE FEARLESS HAMSTER

Start with the earliest facts you know. ←

One of seven

Sherbet was born in a pet shop, but she wasn't born alone. Her Mum had six others — 4 brothers and 2 sisters for Sherbet. She was by far the smallest of all seven, but that wasn't the only different thing about Sherbet — she was completely white and had red eyes, but all of the others, including her Mum, were brown.

Leaving the cage

I remember the first time I saw Sherbet. She was sitting on her back legs, eating a sunflower seed. "That one's an albino," the owner of the pet shop said. I knew then that I had to have her. I paid the six pounds and put my hand into the cage to get her out. She walked onto it as if she already knew me, and I knew I had made the right choice.

Write about one event or achievement in each section.

Escape!

← *Put a new sub-heading for each section.*

Sherbet had been in her new cage for nearly a year, when one day my little sister made a terrible mistake. She left the cage door open, and in her usual inquisitive way, Sherbet thought that she would explore. I can't tell you what she discovered while she was out of the cage, as only she knows, but I can tell you that we searched the house from top to bottom looking for her.

We had all given up searching, and I was feeling miserable when, a week later, when I got home, Mum had a big smile on her face for two reasons. The first reason was that she had bought a replacement for Sherbet — a brown male hamster called Lollipop. But even better, Mum had been in the garden and had discovered a very dirty Sherbet hiding in a plant pot!

You don't have to say what happened on every single day. Concentrate on the most interesting events.

A mum to be!

We thought that Sherbet must have been lonely while I was school and that was why she tried to escape, so we decided to keep Lollipop too. After a few weeks, we had some great news — Sherbet was getting bigger and bigger, and we took her to the vet, who told us she was pregnant.

Sherbet is the best hamster you could ask for — she's brave and clever to survive for so long outside, and now she's going to be a mum too!

Finish by summing up how you feel about whoever you're writing about.

Newsletters

A good newsletter should make readers stop whatever they're doing, and pay attention. You've got to make your event sound like the place they simply <u>have</u> to be.

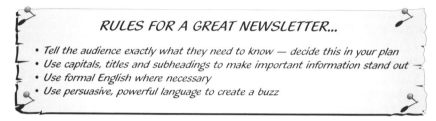

RULES FOR A GREAT NEWSLETTER...

• *Tell the audience exactly what they need to know — decide this in your plan*
• *Use capitals, titles and subheadings to make important information stand out*
• *Use formal English where necessary*
• *Use persuasive, powerful language to create a buzz*

Here's a SAT-style <u>newsletter</u> question...

St Barnabus Primary School is holding a talent competition.

The Headteacher wants to invite as many parents and members of the community as possible to raise funds for the school.

He has asked the children to promote the competition using a newsletter.

Imagine you are a Year 6 pupil at the school.

Your task is to write a newsletter promoting the talent contest.

If you're given a writing frame, use it to get your ideas straight before you start.

> *Think about what people reading the newsletter will <u>want</u> to know and what they will <u>need</u> to know.*

When is it happening? *Friday 21st March in the school hall*

Where is it happening? *school hall*

Who is invited? *parents, local people, governors, a mystery guest*

What will happen at the event?	**Why** should parents come?
Singing, dancing, joke-telling, magic — performed by children of all ages *Raffle and tombola* *A celebrity guest* *A barbecue and disco afterwards*	*To see their children perform* *To meet the celebrity* *To win prizes* *To raise money for the school* *To have fun*

Newsletters

Put together the <u>plan</u> and the <u>rules</u> and you should get something like this.
The main points are from the **WHAT** and **WHY** parts of the writing frame.

Put the most important information at the beginning.

ROCK YOUR SOCKS OFF
AT ST BARNABUS'S 'STARS IN THEIR EYES' TALENT CONTEST

You are invited to support the excellent work
at St. Barnabus Primary School by coming along to our rocking

'STARS IN THEIR EYES' TALENT CONTEST!

If you want something to stand out, put it in capitals.

It starts at 5.30pm on Friday 21st March in the school hall.
Don't let us down — show your face around!

EVENTS

Use sub-headings to split the information into clear chunks.

Children from every class will be singing, dancing, juggling, telling jokes or doing magic tricks for your pleasure. The children have worked very hard preparing their acts, so why not come along and give them all your support?
There will also be a raffle and tombola with gifts donated from many famous sources. There are refreshments and a barbeque and disco after the show hosted by our mystery celebrity guest!

Make the language quite formal — like a real letter from your school to your parents.

PRIZES

There are many prizes to be won by the children for taking part, but also for any adults who want to sing for us or perhaps tell a few jokes.

Mention anything that will help persuade mums and dads to come along.

FUND RAISING

All money made will go towards a tremendous trip for our Year 6 pupils at the end of their SATs. They are working very hard for the good name of our school so all donations, no matter how small, will be most welcome.
So why not come along and join the fun?

Put any really vital information at the beginning <u>and</u> the end.

'STARS IN THEIR EYES' TALENT CONTEST!
5.30pm Friday 21st March

Instructions

Good instructions make even quite difficult things seem easy.
The trick is to break everything down into clear, simple steps.

RULES FOR GREAT INSTRUCTIONS...

- *Write a new instruction for each different thing you have to do*
- *Number, or bullet point, each instruction*
- *Make each step clear and easy to understand*
- *Put the steps in the right order*
- *Always re-read the finished instructions to check they make sense*

Here's a SAT-style question asking you to **write instructions**...

Imagine that a friend is coming to your house for tea and basketball practice. He or she hasn't lived in the area long and needs to know how to get to your house.

Write out some instructions that your friend can understand.
You will need to decide:

- Where your friend is coming from
- How many steps to break up the instructions into
- What language to use to make the instructions clear

Plan what to say in your instructions before you write them.

How should your friend get to your house?

She will start at Weirdwell Primary School and finish up at 5 Cawdor Lane.
She'll be on foot.

How many steps will the instructions break up into?

Ten or less to keep it simple.

How will you **separate** each step of the instructions?

Every time she has to turn I will write a new instruction.

What kind of language will you use? ....*very simple and clear language so it's*
.easy to understand.................

© CGP 2003

Instructions

If you stick to the rules, you should now be able to write some cracking instructions.
Remember to keep them super-clear.

> In the title, say what the
> instructions are for.

INSTRUCTIONS FOR GETTING FROM SCHOOL TO 5 CAWDOR LANE

1) Leave school by the door and go to the gate. ◄ | Start with the very first step.

2) When you've gone through the gate, turn right. ◄ | Write a new step every time
   there's a new instruction.

3) Go straight on over two roads until you get to Macduff Street.

4) Turn right again onto Macduff Street.

5) Keep going up Macduff Street until you reach the end. | Mention anything that
   could be tricky and say
   how to deal with it.

6) At the top of Macduff Street is Ross Avenue. Cross at the traffic
   lights (you usually have to wait ages before the green man is showing).

7) Turn left and go past the shops
   ('Afro Archies Hairdresser's' and 'We Fry It, You Buy It' chip shop).

8) Our road is the next left — the sign says Cawdor Lane.

9) Our house is halfway down the street on your right, just after the postbox
   (the one that has a splodge of green paint on it).

10) We live in the upstairs flat so when you get to the front door of number 5
    you have to ring the top door bell. ◄ | Make your instructions detailed
    right up to the very end.

   Have you got all that? Right, I'll see you tonight for tea.
   Mum is making your favourite, macaroni cheese — nice!!

> Imagine you had to use your
> instructions — would they be helpful?

> These instructions are for a friend,
> so you can be quite informal.

 Instructions

Descriptions

*A good description will make the reader feel as if they can
actually <u>see</u> the thing you're describing in front of them.*

RULES FOR A GREAT DESCRIPTION...

- *Use descriptions in part of your writing or make the whole thing a description*
- *Mention every part of whatever you're describing*
- *Pay special attention to anything that's different
  or unusual about the thing you're describing*
- *Write descriptions that use all five senses — sight, touch, hearing,
  smell and taste*

Here's a SAT-style <u>description</u> question...

Your parents want to meet your teacher at the school sports day,
but they're not sure what he or she looks like.

**Write a description of your teacher, so your parents
can easily recognise him or her. Include appearance
and personality in your description.**

You will need to think about:

- What your teacher looks like
- Your teacher's personality
- How to help your parents imagine
  exactly what your teacher looks like

Make a plan before you write the description.

Who are you writing about? *Mr. Jones, my teacher*......................................

What does he or she **look** like?

*Don't just describe their face
— think about their build,
clothes and colouring.*

*Tall, thin, nearly bald, pointy face with green eyes.
Always wears the same suit and socks.*

What is his or her **personality** like?

*Think of interesting things that make
them different from anyone else.*

*Strict, doesn't smile much. Doesn't like talking to people much
(unless it's about stamps) and doesn't like sport.*

© CGP 2003

Descriptions

Use your plan and the rules to write a description something like this. Put yourself in the reader's shoes — what would help them picture the person you're describing?

Write about something different in each paragraph.

Mr. Jones

Mr. Jones is very tall and thin — about three times as tall as me. He is almost bald, but has a small strip of hair that he carefully places over the top of his head. Sometimes, when it's windy, this piece of hair becomes unstuck and flops down over his eyes and nearly reaches his chin. From what I can tell (there isn't much to see), his hair is browny-black and very greasy.

He has a very pointy chin and yellowy-green eyes that remind me a bit of snake's eyes. He is always scratching his neck, and when he does, you'll notice that he has really long fingernails. If you're very close to him (I wouldn't be if I were you), you'll hear the loud, scraping sound of his nails across his skin.

Cover all the senses in your descriptions.

He always wears the same brown suit. It smells slightly of egg sandwiches, and generally needs a good iron. The trouser legs are a tiny bit too short for him and so you can see his socks, which will either be bright red or bright green — I think he only owns two pairs, which he swaps over each week.

Write about the things that make whatever you're describing different or unusual.

He is very strict and doesn't smile much. When he does, he only smiles with the left side of his face, which makes him look less friendly than when he's not smiling. I don't think he likes talking to people much, but if you get him talking about his stamp collection then he'll be fine — that's about the only time he ever looks excited, actually.

At the sports day he's unlikely to be helping out with the races, as I don't think he approves of sport. He's more likely to be inside, supervising the people who have been naughty and aren't allowed to join in the races — that's more his cup of tea.

Don't just say what a person looks like — write about what they do and say, too.

Anyway, say hello to him from me when you find him.

Explanations

A good explanation should tell readers all about something — and help them to understand it. Explanations are the type of writing you see in books like science books and encyclopaedias.

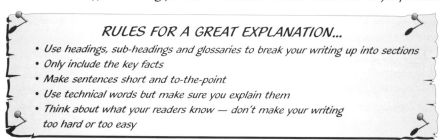

RULES FOR A GREAT EXPLANATION...

- *Use headings, sub-headings and glossaries to break your writing up into sections*
- *Only include the key facts*
- *Make sentences short and to-the-point*
- *Use technical words but make sure you explain them*
- *Think about what your readers know — don't make your writing too hard or too easy*

Here's a SAT-style question asking you to write an explanation...

Year 4 are learning about the water cycle but have lost the class science book that explains how it works.

Write a text that explains the water cycle, using the technical words they need to know.

You will need to decide:

- What the main facts you need to include are
- What technical words to include
- How to lay out your explanation

Always work out what you want to say <u>before</u> you start writing.

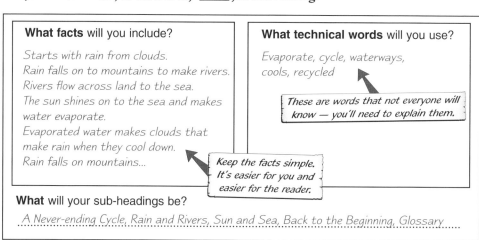

What facts will you include?

*Starts with rain from clouds.
Rain falls on to mountains to make rivers.
Rivers flow across land to the sea.
The sun shines on to the sea and makes water evaporate.
Evaporated water makes clouds that make rain when they cool down.
Rain falls on mountains...*

What technical words will you use?

Evaporate, cycle, waterways, cools, recycled

These are words that not everyone will know — you'll need to explain them.

Keep the facts simple. It's easier for you and easier for the reader.

What will your sub-headings be?

A Never-ending Cycle, Rain and Rivers, Sun and Sea, Back to the Beginning, Glossary

© CGP 2003

Explanations

*Once you're sure what facts you want to explain, you can
concentrate on helping your readers to understand.*

---

*Start with a title that
Year 4s will understand.* → <u>Where Does All our Water Come From?</u>

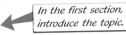

*In the first section,
introduce the topic.*

<u>A Never-ending Cycle</u>

Water is everywhere. It fills oceans, rivers, lakes and ponds. It comes out of our taps for
us to drink and to keep us clean. It is all around us all the time, but did you know that it
is recycled? That's right!

Our water is continually being evaporated by the sun, cooled and then rained into our
rivers again for everyone on the planet to use again and again. It's called the water cycle
and this is how it works...

*Write in a simple, friendly
way for younger people.*

<u>Rain and Rivers</u>

Everyday it rains somewhere in the world. The world needs rain for plants and drinking
water. Rain comes from clouds that float above the earth. When rains falls onto the
ground, it flows into streams and rivers. These waterways run across countries and are
used by humans and animals. At the end of their journey they fill the oceans of the
world.

*Put a new sub-heading for each
new part of the explanation.*

<u>Sun and Sea</u>

When the sun shines on the water in the sea it heats it up which makes it evaporate.
When it evaporates, the water floats up into the sky as a gas and makes clouds.

<u>Back to the Beginning</u>

Eventually the water in the clouds cools down again. When it cools, it falls as rain, onto
the ground to fill the rivers and so on. The water cycle never stops. It happens night and
day around the world. In fact it's happening right now!

*Explain <u>all</u> the technical
words in the glossary.*

<u>Glossary</u>

Evaporate:	When water is heated up it turns from a liquid into a gas. When it cools down it turns back into water.
Cycle:	Something that happens again and again without stopping.
Cools:	When something warm gets slowly colder, it cools.
Recycled:	If something is recycled, it is used again even if it has been thrown away.
Waterway:	Any stream or river that carries water to the oceans.